To Melissa,

Who taught me everything I know about video. I love you.

Jeremy

# HOW TO MAKE A
# PROFESSIONAL VIDEO
## IN 7 STEPS

### Jeremy Wood

#### Cinematic Visions

www.CinematicVisions.com

# Table of Contents

# Introduction

If you're in the business of business, have a website or are on social media - you know the power of video. Pretty much everyone who is anyone uses it. Big companies, little companies, influencers, and just people trying to share something from their lives – all use video. Why? Because it simply is the closest thing to "being there," allowing someone to hear your voice, or see what you're trying to convey. Text is good, photos are better, but simply put video is best.

Do a quick search on Google as to why your company should be using video to market itself. You'll be inundated with ever increasing numbers of search results and studies stating how if you're not using video – you're being left behind. It says something that marketing companies have paid so much money to research the effectiveness of video on those who consume it, and why they do so.

Go ahead. Take a few minutes and go look.

*(Elevator / On Hold Music)*

Welcome back! Now that you know why video is regarded as one of, if not THE most important tool in a person's marketing toolbox, the next question is: "Are you using it?" If you are, does it reflect your company's standard of quality? Does it effectively communicate your message? Are people seeing it, interacting with it, sharing it? In short, does it work?

If you're not using video, why? Are you fearful you can't answer the questions from the previous paragraph? Are you not sure where to start? Do you not have the time? Are you worried about budget? All these questions are valid – but they have answers that are easy to overcome.

First, if you have the budget, and have no time – find a company that you can trust to help you create the video you have in mind (Shameless Plug: If you don't know of one – might I suggest me? I'm easy to reach – you can start here: www.cinematicvisions.com). Sometimes it's simply better to stick to what you're good at, focus on those things, and let someone else handle the other stuff. But let's say you're a DIY'er, you like to learn new things, or perhaps you have no budget – and you really want to jump in the wave of videos that people are using more and more each day to reach potential customers. That's what this book is for. Having been in the video business since 2003, I've learned what it takes to make a video that will not only look good, but also be effective in reaching your audience. Instead of learning the way I did (sometimes by fire), let me walk you through the process I've crafted over the years in order to make my clients happy with what I've done, bring them customers, and make video production a little more easy to digest. It's a 7 Step Process that is tried and true and will work for you whether you're making a marketing / promotional video, a training and safety video, or just something creative. This will help you cut down on the amount of work you'll have to go through while creating the video, keep everyone involved on the same page, lead you to a finished video that matches your vision, and then I'll throw in a bonus 8th step to show you how to make sure your video is seen (because what good is a beautiful car without an engine?).

So, without further ado, here are my "7 Steps to Creating a Professional Video," with the Bonus 8th Step:

1. Pre-Production
2. Scripting
3. Shot Listing / Story Boarding
4. Production
5. Post-Production
6. Delivery
7. Distribution
8. BONUS STEP: Ad Campaigns

If you've been in the business of video creation – most, if not all these steps and the terminology will sound familiar. Even if you're not familiar with video production – these steps shouldn't be too hard to understand. Each step has several components to it that will make creating a video much easier. As I break down each step on the following pages, I'll go into detail as to what you should be doing in each step, suggested equipment to utilize, and tips that I've learned that can help you cut a few corners on budget. Are you ready? If so, let's get into Pre-Production, what that means, and how to get it done.

## Step 1: Pre-Production

The term Pre-Production is self-explanatory and sounds simple, but this one step is as important as any of the steps. There's a Bible verse that says: "Without vision – the people perish." I'm sure no one will perish if you don't get this step right (unless you're working with some really difficult people), but I can safely say that if you don't take this step seriously and make sure everyone is on the same page before proceeding – your project will grow exponentially more difficult as you proceed. This is where everyone involved on your team and / or the team you're working for must come together and agree on what this video is going to convey and how it will ultimately look. Everything from the content, the length of the video, the vision or objective of the video, and where and how it will be used – potentially all the way down to the music you use (though things like music, graphics, fonts, etc., can be determined in production and post production). This step starts as brainstorming, but at the end of the meeting(s), there should be a clear image in everyone's mind as to how this video is going to look.

It's important that anyone and everyone with a say is involved in this step, and that everyone has signed off on the agreed upon concept. When I say "signed off," I mean after the meeting(s), put it all into painfully detailed notes that you can share - allow everyone to review them and make any changes, and once it's all "finalized" literally make everyone sign or approve the document and send it back to you if you can. If you do this, you will have in writing from the get-go that what you end up creating is exactly what everyone agreed to. Of course, if you're creating this video for yourself, there's no need for all of this. But if you're a video production company or working for a company that has put you in charge of the project – this will be helpful if people start trying to change things midstream on you. Sometimes those changes are needed. But any time the original plan is deviated from – add that to your notes and get everyone's buy in! Protect yourself through the process.

As for the video itself, this is where everyone talks about what they see playing on their mind's movie screen. Discuss what issue is being overcome with this video. What's worked with customers in the past? What are your competitors or similar companies in other markets doing? Identify the problem, the pain and the solution. Talk about any calls to action that will grab people's attention. What can you offer that will perhaps motivate people to act on what they see? It is in this stage where anything and everything related to the topic can be discussed. Do you need an actor or actress, or several? Can you get by with just a voice over? Will there be any audible voices in the video, or will it be primarily graphics, animations, or stock photos and stock video? Are you even addressing a problem in this video and asking people to act? Or is it a branding video that simply tells people who you are and what you do? Do you want it to be funny, sad, emotional, or informative? Since you haven't done anything – this is where all ideas can be explored. By the end of the meeting(s) however, a clear vision should emerge and everyone should put aside their feelings in order to achieve a consensus on what the video will look like and what it is intended to accomplish. Anything that was a great idea but ended up "not making the cut" so to speak, should be filed away for a potential video down the road. If not for this company, then for yourself when presenting or considering ideas in the future.

This is Pre-Production. It is where the idea is birthed and vetted for its quality. Remember, before proceeding to any further steps – this must all be agreed on. How do you write a script if no one agrees on what the video should be? How do you film when there is no consensus on what or who should be in front of the camera? As I mentioned at the beginning of this section – this step might be the most important. It certainly sets the tone and lays out the foundation for what is to come. If you move forward with dissenting opinions or "wet paint" you will find yourself going back to the drawing board over and over. So, get everyone at the starting line and finding the finish line will be so much easier.

TIP:

If you're in charge of this pre-production meeting, try to maintain control and keep people on track as best as possible. Allow people to express themselves and think big but keep the conversation on track. Don't let people start going in different directions – unless that's where the video is headed, as new ideas emerge. The tendency is that people start thinking of things that are unrelated and time ends up getting wasted. Again, I'm not saying shut every idea down, but be attentive to times where you can feel things slipping away. It's important to keep everyone on topic – especially if you're a production company or working for a company. Time is money – and every minute burned talking about things that have nothing to do with your end-result is cutting into your profit, or theirs. Which brings me to the meeting or meetings themselves. Set a time and stick to it. If you've set aside an hour – stay true to that. If you don't stick to the schedule from the beginning – then you are setting the expectation from the start that time is not important. I'm not saying to be a jerk, or look at your watch every 10 minutes, but do your best to be respectful of everyone's time and they'll be respectful of yours in return. Get everywhere early and be ready to start at the appointed time, and if possible, work in a way that gets everyone out early or on time. The example you set will be followed, even if your customers must come around to it. Be polite and professional - and being on time is one of the best ways to do that.

## Step 2: Scripting

Now that everyone has agreed to what the video will look like, what its purpose is, and how to proceed – it's time to write the script. This can be a hard spot for people to get moving on, because the hardest thing to do in starting the script is nailing the beginning. How do you start? What should you say? A lot of time is spent staring at an empty screen as your brain tries to come up with an Academy Award winning opening. Hopefully, some of this will have been solved in your Pre-Production meetings – but putting it into words can be difficult. My suggestion (as simple as this sounds) is just get started. Start typing. What do you see in your mind? Even if it takes 200 words or more to describe it – start typing. An easy way to kick things off though is to just imagine an intro. If you're making a video for your company, band, or project – that often starts with a logo and some music. Start there. A script isn't just the words which are spoken in the video. They are also a description of what is happening.

This brings me to the format for writing a script. While some people might prefer just writing things out in paragraph form – with a sentence or two of what should be on camera – I really like to separate things out with

"Video" and "Audio." In other words, one side of the script is what the viewer hears, the other side (with the corresponding audio) is a description of what is seen on screen as these words, sounds, or music is being played. Here's an example of what I mean.

| VIDEO | AUDIO |
|---|---|
| Intro:<br><br>Logo Animation showing the logo coming up on the screen in a creative way<br><br>Company website appears as the animation is finishing | Intro:<br><br>Music plays as logo appears, lowers in volume as the voice over begins |
| Video shot of frustrated businessman / woman looking at their computer and bills | Voice Over:<br><br>"Are you having a hard time reaching new customers, making each month an uphill battle for you and your business?" |

Two quick things: first, the video section as it's filled out here is an example of shot listing – which we'll get to in the next section. Second, notice that each phase or part of the video and audio is in a new section as it transitions to something new. Again, not everyone will work this way – but I like it in order to keep each element separate. I also like it because I can print the script off and check or "X" off my progress. If you're a "list checker" or someone who likes to chart your progress, you'll like this. If this seems like an odd way to create a script to you, find a way that helps you understand each and everything you're doing – just be sure you can show it to your client or team and it's not like solving a puzzle just to figure it out. Just like the Pre-Production step, you need to get everyone to sign off with their approval of the script. It also makes it easier to break the video down into sections, making it easier to transition from topic to topic and keep everything organized and separated.

One final reason I like this format is because once the shot list is filled in, not only do you essentially have a checklist to go by for filming or graphics creation, etc., the script is now what I term "visually descriptive." In other words, as the reader is going over the audio, they can look at the description of what will be on the screen with the video, and they will begin to "see" the finished product. If that can be accomplished, and if you mind your Ps and Qs while creating those visual elements – they will have basically seen the video before you even begin in earnest. I'll reiterate this in the shot listing section, but I wanted you to understand why this format can be so helpful for both your clients and you.

Now for the script itself – remember – you are telling a story. Make it interesting and understandable. Find a way to put yourself in the viewer's mind and write something that will make it relatable. Avoid industry jargon or terms that won't make sense to someone who knows what they need, but don't know what to call it. Think of all the times you've had something go wrong with your computer, your car, or your furnace and you need help. How frustrating is it to try to find someone who will talk in terms that make sense to you, so you feel comfortable that they aren't just selling you something that costs a lot of money while you're not even sure what it is? This is the script you need to be thinking of. We all know that sometimes you only get one chance to make a first impression, so remember that when writing the script. Videos are virtual handshakes with your customers or viewers. They are a chance – sometimes the only chance you'll have – to show them who you are, what you do, and how you can help them. Construct your words in that way.

If you're working to create a promotional or marketing video for a company, and you're not familiar with them – of course you can use their marketing materials and website to begin to construct a script, but sometimes you need it boiled down. So, don't be afraid to ask for a list of 10 to 15 bullet points that you can build the script around. You may even need to have them sit down with you and assist in the writing of the script. There's no shame in that. Afterall, they know their company backward and forward, and asking for their expertise is not taboo. The advantages of that further allows them into the scripting process, which allows them to again know exactly what the video is going to say and look like. DON'T FORGET: Get everyone's approval at this stage as well!

TIP 1:

Every video should have a beginning, middle, and end. Each step is the most important as the video progresses, but if there is a step that is perhaps the most important – it's the beginning. Most studies show that people will have turned a video off within the first 15 to 30 seconds. Therefore, you must put something in front of them to make them want to see the middle and end of the video. So, work these sections out with your team, but make sure your start to the video looks like a hook with a big, fat, juicy worm to a fish. Make it compelling.

Usually it will start like this...Beginning: Introduce the problem. Do this with a question if you can. For example: "Are you having trouble with XYZ?", "Does XYZ always seem to trip you up?", "Have you ever had this problem?" The reason a question is important is it grabs the customers' attention – you have done something right out of the gate that they can relate to. If you are a business that provides a solution to a potential pain in the rear end for people – then you need them nodding their head in agreement from the start. Asking that question tells them right off the bat that you know the problem, are familiar with it, and a solution is on the way.

Next up is the Middle. This is where you show the customer how this problem is hurting them or keeping them from getting their desired result. You can do this by continuing to ask questions, or just outlining all the known issues surrounding the problem. For instance, if someone is having a hard time reaching customers, I might start the video with the question, "Are you having a hard time reaching customers?" Then the middle will address the issues with that problem, with something like, "If you can't reach customers, you can't grow, and if you can't grow how will you ever reach your goals?" Something like that. You're addressing the problem in the beginning of the video, the pain associated with that problem in the middle, and then finally in the end of the video you're providing the solution and what you do. Which might say something along the lines of, "If this describes what you're business is struggling with – then contact Cinematic Visions and allow us to create and distribute a video that will help you not only reach customers, but have them contacting you for your services!" In the end, you can even throw in some sort of Call to Action, such as, "Mention this video for 10% off of your video," or "Go online today and contact us for your FREE no obligation consultation!"

In all of this, keep in mind what most studies show and suggest for the length of your video. Social Media videos really shouldn't go too much past 30 seconds. But if need be, 2 to 3 minutes would be the longest you should create. Website videos can be in the 2 to 3-minute range, but again not too much longer. If you have a long video – consider trying to break it into smaller, more digestible pieces for people. Believe it or not, people are more likely to watch 10, 1-minute videos than one 6 to 7-minute video. So, look for ways to create a video that is short and to the point, and remember – hook them in that first 15 to 30 seconds! If you have a captivated audience, such as at a convention or some sort of presentation – of course consult with the people hosting the event. But I still wouldn't do a video that is much more than 5 to 7-minutes, even in that case. The reasons being is that it is hard to create a video that is compelling all the way through when it's that long, and more and more we are learning people's attention spans just can't handle too much more (unless you've got super powers and are fighting off bad guys).

TIP 2:

Sometimes a video is a testimonial. In this case you can script out what you want people to say, provide them bullet points to help them shape their thoughts, or just let them wing it. In any case, if this is what your video is going to be – writing a script is a bit different. Your script design serves more as a guide or outline for what people are going to say. Shot listing for this can be pre-planned a bit – which we will go over in the next section, but you might have to do it after you've heard what people say on camera. If this is the type of video you're creating – don't let your subject ramble on forever. Remember, the video still needs to move and be compelling. If you don't script out what they are going to say, help them keep it short and sweet!

# Step 3: Shot Listing / Story Boarding

I've already touched on this a little bit in the previous section, but after you've created the words or script that are going to be used in the video – you need some visuals to go with them. This is what shot listing is. In some circles this is also called "Story Boarding." In some cases – actual storyboards are created with computer generated or artist renderings which sort of look like cartoons or images to visually show what the shot on the screen will look like. However, I've found that in most cases a well worded description of what you're planning to have appear on the screen will suffice.

As I mentioned when discussing scripting, try to break the script down into sections. So, when a paragraph or topic ends, you basically end the "box" or row and move on. Again, this helps know what should appear on the screen for that voice over, or scene in the video, making it easier to chart your progress and transition from one scene to the next.

When writing or describing the video portion with the corresponding audio portion – be as visually descriptive as possible. Think of the shot list as the director's, cinematographer's and editor's (which might all be you) instructions on how to create the video you're outlining. For example, don't just write "guy looking at computer." Paint a better picture, use emotions, angle descriptions, pacing, and whether the camera will be moving or still. I've listed at the end of this section some terms, definitions and abbreviations to help. Getting back to our guy looking at the computer a better description would be: "Mid shot of a businessman looking at his computer. He is visibly frustrated, as he looks at the screen and a pile of bills next to him, as the camera zooms closer to his face." That description tells us exactly what we need to know. We've all either been that guy, or we've seen him. Now the people looking over your script know what the shot will look like. They've basically seen it in their mind's eye. Of course, the final shot might not match perfectly (especially if you're using stock footage) – but they won't be thrown off with what you've placed in the video. IF you've gotten everyone to sign off on the pre-production, the script and now your shot list – when they see the video – they won't be shocked or confused by what you've done. They will have essentially not only seen it already – but approved it. So much easier!

Going back to the scripting portion a little, the words / script you've placed in the audio portion of your script should make writing out a shot list easy. If what is written there doesn't automatically allow you to describe what you want on the screen – then you need to go back to the audio portion of the script and re-think it. If the script says, "make sure you stop completely at a stop sign," you know what you need to show on the screen. If it's not clear you're going to have a hard time finding footage for that or trying to film something to fit. So, be descriptive on both sides of the script. All of this might seem like a lot of work, as we're only in the third step and we haven't even begun to film, edit or design, but believe me – the hard work and time put into these steps are extremely important and will save you so many headaches when you begin the process of actual creation. A final benefit of doing the shot list is that you will only need to film / create what is on that list. There's nothing worse that showing up to film something and not knowing exactly what you need, whether it be the main shots or just b-roll / secondary shots. A shot list ensures you only film what you need and aren't needlessly filming a bunch of things that will never be used. That's not a good use of anyone's time. Making an approved shot list just streamlines everything. This is not to say you can't do a few extra things once on set if something presents itself and would work – but this will keep you on track. It also helps you keep a client who is trying to milk you for everything they can stay within the confines of what was agreed to. If your contract is done right – then the shot list is part of what they're paying you for. If they start asking for more than what they agreed to in the contract, script and shot list – you're able to legitimately charge more without feeling bad. Take the time to do these steps thoroughly and REMEMBER! Get everyone to sign off!

If you are interested in storyboarding with actual images, you can also find an artist to draw what you need, or you can search google images or royalty free stock images to create actual images to better illustrate what you want to create. This can be time consuming, but sometimes it will be needed for your clients. Again, a well worded description has always worked for me, but I have the confidence I could do both if needed, and so should you!

TIPS:

Here are some terms, definitions and descriptions that will help you with making a more effective shot list.

Close Up / Close Shot / Extreme Close Up – Kind of easy to understand, but it usually features something up close (obviously), such as a face, hand, object – with little or nothing else in the shot.

Mid Shot / Cowboy Shot – This is a shot that might include a person from the waist or knees up, or even an object. In the shot might be other items that help to tell the story or affirm the setting.

Wide Shot / Long Shot – This shot would perhaps include a person from head to toe, or an object, along with their surroundings.

Head Shot – No, this is not a punch or anything else to the head! This simply refers to the person's head, or head and shoulders being in the shot.

Aerial Shot – Overhead, either from a drone, plane, helicopter or even a crane.

Establishing Shot – A shot that "sets the scene." Most of the time these would be shots from a distance showing a town, or something from afar to establish where and when the story is taking place.

Handheld Shot – This denotes that the camera will not be on a tripod, but rather in the hands of the filmmaker. These can be used to create a more organic feel, or even an uneasy feeling as the camera is harder to hold still. If you're a fan of "The Office," much of that show was handheld.

Low Angle Shot – This is when the camera is positioned lower, looking up at a figure / character / object, to give the impression of intimidation or to make something look bigger.

High Angle Shot – A camera from high above the figure / character / object to help give the impression of a smaller size, helplessness, joy or just used as an establishing shot.

Locked Down Shot – The camera here is positioned on a tripod and not moved at all during the scene.

Money Shot – Often the most expensive, most important shot in the video to really drive home the point.

Over the Shoulder Shot – The camera is positioned over the speaker's shoulder or a person who is listening to a speaker, which is extremely helpful in connecting the audience with the person speaking, or the person listening.

Pan – This is when the camera moves left to right or right to left.

Tilt – The camera moves from up to down, or down to up.

POV – Point of View. The shot depicts what the character being featured is seeing from his or her perspective.

Tracking Shot – A shot where the camera follows from behind or alongside the subject on screen.

Zoom – Using a variable lens to move in or push out without moving the camera.

Crane Shot – The camera is attached to a crane or jib crane in this shot and moved really in almost any direction.

These are just a few terms you can use in describing your shot – of course if you want to find more, or if something you're trying to do isn't described here – simply do a search on Google and you'll find multiple lists with a lot more to help you learn how to speak in film terms.

# Step 4: Production

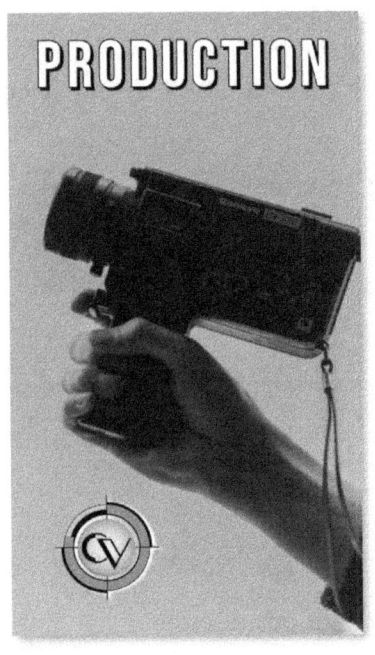

Finally. If you've done everything you should in steps 1 through 3, you are ready to start filming, doing graphic design, creating animations, picking music – all of it. It's time to produce the video you've been brainstorming, scripting, and shot listing. One warning – if you have not taken the time to get everyone signed off and on board with the first 3 steps, stop now and get that done. Don't start creating a video without your team's approval. This will save you countless minutes and hours of re-filming and re-doing things. It's important to note that this step might not actually require you to film anything. There are a ton of royalty free stock footage and photo websites out there, where you can subscribe or purchase the products they offer. In this section, however, I'm going to concentrate on filming – I'll go over stock footage and photos in section 5 where we discuss post-production – since these services are just download and go.

Once your shot list is approved this is what you're going to work on now. Here's where the video can go in a million different directions, depending on what you've put together in your first 3 steps. So, it's hard to be specific here in telling you how to create the video. But I'll go through a few scenarios and provide some options for you for filming, creating, searching for and utilizing stock footage and photos, etc.

The first one we'll go over is filming. Perhaps you've done this before, you have an expensive camera, sound and lighting equipment, and you pretty much know what you're doing here – if so – great! Get to it. But if you're new to this process, let me go over some ways you can film and create a nice-looking video, with high production values, without tons of money invested in equipment.

CAMERA OPTIONS

Let's start with your phone. If you have a decent iPhone, or a newer android phone, like the Samsung models – then you have a camera that can produce wonderful images. If you search the internet or YouTube, you can find stunning videos that have been produced by these phones. And with a little practice – you can produce videos that look just fine for the purposes of marketing yourself or someone else, combined with an editing software or app, that allows you to edit the video, create graphics, add music and so on. Professional cameras, and DSLRs are also in consideration here. As each one can be very different from the other – I won't go into all the functions they have – and what they do. But if you're using something along these lines – the best thing to do is to get out and use it. Practice with it – a lot. Find online tutorials. Press all the buttons and figure out what they do, and what they're for. If you're not sure what something means – look it up. A simple search online will help you to understand your equipment and what it is capable of!

No matter what camera you're using it is important to set it properly for the correct resolution and frames per second. Most cameras nowadays are high definition. The most common format is 1920x1080p, and either 29.97 frames per second (fps) or 30 fps – these settings will be fine for nearly any video you create. If you want a more cinematic look, try shooting in 23.976 fps or 24 fps. The slower frame rate creates a softer more film-like look, this is what most major motion pictures are filmed with. If you think of what you see at the theater versus what you see on the local newscasts – this is the difference I'm describing. Films just look like – well film. TV often looks crisper and clearer. So, it's up to you to decide the look you want to achieve. Some phones may not have this option, if not, the 29.97 or 30 will be fine. If you're adventurous and would like to be able to create a "multi-camera" look, and your camera has the capability – switch it to 4K. When you're in the editing / post production phase you can set your editing software to a smaller resolutions, such as 1920x1080p, and with your footage technically being 4 times larger – you can crop the image to different sections of your shot, create zooms, pans and tilts – a lot of cool stuff! If you want to try that – but aren't sure how to – you can set up a consultation / training with me, and I can show you how, just contact me through my website at www.cinematicvisions.com. Or you can try to find a tutorial on YouTube for free. It sounds technical and difficult – but it's not hard once you see it in action.

Of course, if you don't have a professional camera, and you don't want to use a phone – there are plenty of options out there, that won't make you cry when you see their prices. I will include a link to my Amazon Storefront later where I've created equipment lists to help you get started – no matter what your level is.

Once you decide on a camera, and what resolution you're going to film in, it's time to talk about the best practices for filming in order to acquire footage that will allow you to make the best video. We'll start with filming a person talking or a subject, and how to make it look good.

FRAMING

When filming a person talking or a dog walking, or anything really, the tendency for most people is to center the person in the middle of the screen. While this is fine for some purposes, such as a live interview on the news, for a more professional look I like to use the "Rule of Thirds" when filming someone, or something. If you're filming with a phone in most cases you will want to film with the phone turned sideways to achieve the look we're all familiar with on our TVs, and most videos online. However, if you're filming for Instagram, or other social media outlets which require a squared look, you may want to turn it straight up and down. Just consider where the video will be seen most, and what look you want to accomplish. We'll talk more about this in steps 5 and 6.

Here is a simple definition for the Rule of Thirds, from StudioBinder.com:

"The **Rule of Thirds** is the process of dividing an image into **thirds**, using two horizontal and two vertical lines. This imaginary grid yields nine parts with four intersection points. When you position the most important elements of your image at these intersection points, you produce a much more natural image."

Here is an image illustrating what that looks like:

In looking at this photo, you can see the woman is positioned in the left third of the screen. In most cases, it just creates a more visually pleasing composition. The nice thing about producing a video or really anything in the world of creative work – is that it's always up to the artist. This is just what I prefer, and now that I've shown it to you – I bet you'll start seeing it in nearly every video you see! Practice it before you press record and see what you like. Another suggestion I have is don't leave too much headroom. By this I mean, don't place the person's head at the bottom of the screen, leaving a ton of space over the top of them. Always try to place them on the lines you see in the picture I've shared with you and create nice even spacing for your subject on the screen. Also, make sure the background isn't distracting. You don't want a plant to appear to be growing out of your subject's head!

LIGHTING

Once you've positioned your subject where you want them, the next step in creating a professional video is the lighting. Simply using the lighting in a room (which is often overhead, or off to the side), will leave the person in shadow, and can make the final image look dull or flat. Sometimes this can be done to create a mood, or might be the look you want, but for a promotional video, testimonial video or something along those lines – it will always look better to have even lighting across a person's face. Use your eyes. If it looks nice and even, you've done your job. Lookout for hotspots or places where your subject is too dark. For instance, a bright spot on their forehead, and a giant shadow on their neck or under their chin. If you really want to check for these things, some cameras or field monitors have an option that will place "zebra" stripes across the image so you can make it as even as possible. If you can't get a camera or field monitor with these options – again – use your eyes. Try to create an image with as little shadow on the person's face as possible or at least make sure the lighting is smooth, as well as on the walls behind them. Another helpful tip would be to film a little test footage, and then play it back on a computer, or monitor, to see how it looks. Do whatever you have to do to make sure it looks the way you need it to, before officially starting, and finding out after the fact that it won't work!

Once again, there are ways to do this that will help you without breaking the bank. I've included a link to my Amazon Storefront where I have lists created to help you with selecting equipment, including lights – based on your budget and what you're trying to accomplish:

https://www.amazon.com/shop/cinematicv

There are also many other ways to be creative with lighting without a light kit. Using inexpensive equipment such as reflectors and diffusers with natural light can often create the look you need. In many cases, you can handmake some equipment. A simple search on YouTube will provide you with all kinds of creative solutions!

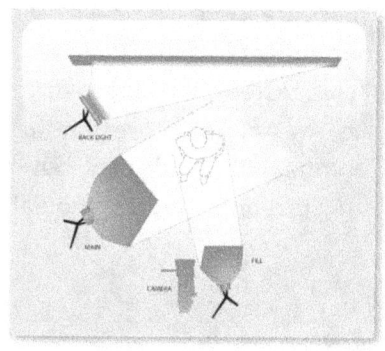

If you do decide to purchase a light kit to help your videos look better or are just making do with what you have, here is a diagram that helps you create ideal lighting for a simple interview, using 3 lights (provided by B&H Photo). Like so many things in video, however, I'd suggest playing around with your setup. Move things around and check your footage to find the look you need.

For more information:
https://www.bhphotovideo.com/explora/video/tips-and-solutions/lighting-interviews

SOUND

I know this book is all about utilizing a process to create a more professional video – but maybe even more important than how your video looks is how it sounds. Research indicates that people will watch a video if the quality of the video is poor, but the sound is comprehendible. On the flip side of that, studies indicate that people will not watch a highly produced video if the sound is bad. Think about your own viewing habits when watching videos. You'll most likely watch a live stream of someone preaching, teaching or telling jokes if you can hear them, even if the video quality is not all that great. But turn that scenario around, where you have a clean, crisp image, but you can't hear or understand what the person is saying. Will you still watch? Most would say no. So, when creating your video, you should put just as much effort into the sound of the video, as you would in the framing and lighting. To do that, you need a microphone. There are millions of microphones to choose from out there. Some cost as much as a small car, and others are more in line with what most people can afford. Pick one with your budget in mind. Read reviews, see if you can find videos where people have tested them and give you their thoughts on how they worked. Again, my Amazon Storefront has a selection of various microphones of different abilities and costs, but most of them would work for a simple marketing, promotional, testimonial, or training video. Here's the link again:

https://www.amazon.com/shop/cinematicv

There are microphones that work very well with phones, so that you can couple the nice image you create with clean audio. Of course, when you're filming you need to consider the environment you're filming in. Some places are going to be impossible to control background noise. If that adds to the video or is just part of where you're filming – the viewer likely won't mind – if it doesn't take over the video, or person they're trying to listen to. If you need quiet, post signs where you're filming (with permission, of course) alerting people to the fact that you're filming and need them to help in being as silent as possible. Also listen the ambient noise of the location. Is there a refrigerator or cooler making noise? Is the air conditioner making a lot of noise? Can you hear too many things that you feel will be distracting in the finished product? If so, try to eliminate as many of those things as you can. If someone's hired you to do this video for them, they'll likely bend over backwards to help tamp those noises down, as they want the video to be as good as it can be too. Of course, if you're making the video for yourself – then ask yourself if it would be worth it to turn things off, or change locations? You can also search for noise cancelling microphones or microphones that have a limited range, which can help eliminate those issues to a degree. A good wind screen is also important to help prevent "popping of the Ps" when the air from someone talking passes over the mic. These are especially important if you're outside on a windy day – for that see if you can purchase a "dead cat" as they're often called (this is what's pictured on the mic at the start of this section). Finally, mic placement is important. If you're using a clip-on, or lavalier microphone, try to place the mic on your

24

subject around 5 to 10 inches from their mouth, and do your best to hide the cord, by tucking it into their shirt, jacket or clothing. If you're using handheld mics, again the 5 to 10-inch range is fine, just make sure your subject is speaking into the mic. As for shotgun mics, depending on what kind you have – move it around until you get optimal sound, and make sure to keep it out of your shot!

I cannot emphasize how important sound is, and if you're interviewing someone – you may not get a second chance to film again to improve it. So, put on some headphones and test, test, test. Make sure when you hit record that you're getting the sound you need. Listen back to it once you're done filming – while the set is still in place, and make sure it's okay. If not, your entire video might end up being worthless.

STABILIZATION

Another important part of making a video is stabilizing your camera. As I mentioned in the scripting section with the definitions, there are times where doing handheld shots might be required to create a certain look or mood, but for the most part you'll likely want your camera shot steady and stable. This requires a tripod. A good tripod is worth its weight in gold. If you like to have a lot of movement in your shots, such as pans and tilts, then you need a fluid head tripod, which will enable you to move your camera around as smoothly as possible. These are great for live events, such as dance recitals, plays, sports, speakers who move a lot and the like, so you don't have herkie, jerky motion as you try to track the action. They're also terrific for enabling smooth shots for b-roll, and artistic shots that you can lay over a person's voice so your video isn't just a talking head the whole time (we'll talk b-roll next). A good fluid head tripod will only cost around $150.

Let's just say that the videos you're creating are simple interviews or testimonials, and you don't plan on making them too fancy with b-roll or having a lot of motion. For the most part, your shots are going to be "locked down," with the camera being in one spot once you've set it - then you don't need an expensive tripod at all. There are $20 and $30 options out there that will work fine, and there are mounts to add to your tripod (fluid head or no) that will hold your phone or tablet in place fine. For a more professional look, a tripod is a big step forward, and with proper framing, lighting and sound, can round out a nice-looking video. There are also affordable solutions out there that will let you get even more creative in your shots. Such as gimbals, Steadicams, jib cranes and more. Some of the gimbals are even specifically designed for today's phones and can help you create visually beautiful shots.

B-ROLL

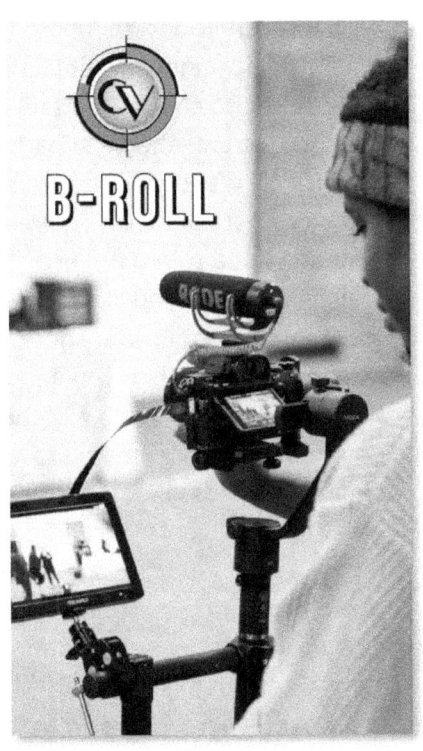

If you want to create a video that looks more polished and highly produced, b-roll is a great way to do that. B-roll is simply a secondary shot, that is often used without sound, and placed over the top of what is considered the primary footage. For example, if you were making a video that was about your business, and your primary shot was you or someone talking to your customers explaining what you do, you might go grab some footage to match what is being discussed in the video. Let's say you're discussing how to make your "widgets," as your voice continues the explanation, a shot replaces your face with some of your widgets being made. B-roll can also work as a transition from one subject to another. Perhaps you're discussing subject A and wrap things up – you could simply place a few artistic shots featuring subject A, or perhaps subject B, and then switch to you talking about that information. The ways you can use b-roll is limited to your imagination. I like to use it to further illustrate the voice over, interview or subject being discussed on the camera, or to just make the overall video more visually appealing.

When you go about filming b-roll try to be creative as well. Film from multiple angles, get close ups, mid shots, wide shots, aerials (if you can), roll your focus back and forth if you can - just let your artistic side take over. Think of shots that would be interesting to see, even if the subject matter isn't all that exciting. I like to challenge myself to make a boring subject seem fascinating and b-roll that presents interesting visuals will keep someone tuned in. If you're a visual person, the b-roll is often the most fun part of filming.

FOCUS

As you can imagine, it is important to make sure the subject / object you're filming is in focus. There are ways to try to sharpen out of focus images in post-production, but in most cases, it won't fix things completely - leaving you with a ruined video, and the need to re-film everything. So, make sure your camera is in focus! A simple way to do this with cameras that have a motorized zoom, where you can press a button in order to zoom in or out, is to simply zoom in on the subject / object you need to be in focus. Next you will press the auto focus button, or manually focus the shot, then switch the camera to manual focus. Now as you zoom back out, your shot will be in focus! Most professionals don't use or trust auto focus, as it can sometimes go in and out – which will ruin a shot. For cameras with an interchangeable lens, where you must manually zoom in or out, frame the shot as you need, then adjust the manual focus until you are satisfied that everything is crystal clear. Just like with listening to audio – as you complete shots – it is always advisable to watch the footage back and make sure it looks just as you intended. It really sucks to leave a location, put your footage into a computer and see that it's out of focus. You'll either have to go back and redo it, find some b-roll to replace it, spend hours trying to fix it or ultimately scrap it. Utilizing a feature on more professional cameras called "peaking" can help, by putting colors on the screen to show what is in focus – though I have found that to not be totally reliable. A better solution is to use a field monitor that is bigger than the LCD screen on your camera – so you can get a better look, and really dial things in.

WHITE BALANCE

This is more technical than the topics before it, but it is important, and if you have the ability – checking your white balance is always a good idea.

White balance is simply trying to match the colors (or color temperature) of the camera's picture to what you see with your eyes. In some instances, you may want to skew that on purpose, but in most cases, you want what you film to look like what you see. If you film with different color temperatures – it will be extremely hard to undo or correct in post-production, which can lead to re-shoots.

A lot of cameras have presets allowing you to click on the option that best matches your situation. If you're filming inside, the white balance won't be the same as if you were outside for instance. Look for these options or see if you can set the color temperature manually (often called Kelvin and symbolized with a K in the settings) to match what you see. In most cases, 3200K to 4000K will work for indoors, and 5600K to 6500K will work for outdoors. If you're not sure, place a white sheet of paper in front of your camera and set the white balance to match the color of the paper. If your camera has an auto white balance option, that can be helpful – but because in some cases the lighting where you're filming changes – the white balance will change as well, causing the colors of your video to shift as you're filming. Correcting this can be a nightmare, and for that reason I usually recommend avoiding the auto white balance option. Again, this is much more technical than the other stuff, but I wanted to at least mention it here as I feel it's important. For more on white balance, and how to use it on your camera – search YouTube for tutorials or google for more information.

RECORDING

This will be short – but after you've done everything you need to do to get the perfect shot and sound – DON'T FORGET TO HIT RECORD!!! I know this seems like a silly warning – but I speak from experience...Hit record and check your footage when you're done. If you are interested in what it feels like to want to crawl into a cave, hide and beat yourself up for a few hours – just skip this step and take the risk – though I would advise against it.

IN CONCLUSION

Production, or the process of creating the content while filming, could probably fill several pages of several books if I really tried to cover each and everything that I've experienced over the years. But these are the basic areas I'd consider the most important.

The best thing I can recommend to you if you really want to get good though, is to go out and practice. Get to know your gear, everything from the camera, the lights, mics and anything else you're using to create the video you're working on. Go online, read and watch tutorials – I've been doing this nearly 20 years and still do that...A lot. Especially if you've been hired or put in charge of creating something for someone. The last thing you want to do is struggle in front of the client while trying to use your own equipment. Again, this is something I've experienced. It's embarrassing and if you're trying to do this for a living, it will destroy the confidence they've placed in you to start with. Keep your camera with you, film around your house, your city, your place of work, inside, outside – wherever you think you might end up filming someday (and keep that footage if it's good – you never know when it might work as b-roll for a project). Lots and lots of practice will make things so much easier when you've experienced what you're trying to accomplish when it's time to get to work. Once again, as with all the previous steps, make sure everyone involved is satisfied with the work done during production. Don't move on until they are!

Suggested Equipment Lists from Cinematic Visions:
https://www.amazon.com/shop/cinematicv

## Step 5: Post-Production

Through the first 4 steps, you've utilized the script and shot list to go through the production process and now it's time to use that same agreed upon document to go through the editing, or post-production process.

At this point, the big question is how are you going to put the video together?

Here are a few options for you to consider, and I will try to list some of the pros and cons with each. Before I go into those areas, keep in mind, that post-production can take just as long – if not considerably longer – than filming or acquiring your assets in the production step.

I've heard it said that when watching a video – you can assume that the editor put in one hour for each edited minute you see. Based on my personal experience sometimes, one hour is way short of the amount of time I spent editing. On simpler, smaller videos one hour is way too much. But if you're a beginner, it will take a while to get it all figured out. If you stick with it though, it can be rewarding and a lot of fun.

Let's start with an editing program. There are different levels of software programs available to you. Some offer professional abilities and are the exact same things Hollywood uses when creating movies, others are intended more for mid-level editors and people just starting out. As you can imagine – the pro level programs can be quite expensive and complex. Some of the programs you may come across are Adobe Premier Pro, Vegas Pro, Avid, and Final Cut Pro. Each offer advantages and disadvantages over the other, it'll be up to you to research each one and determine what you believe will suit your needs. Personally, I use Vegas Pro and Adobe Premier Pro, along with Adobe After Effects. All can produce professional videos. Obviously, these types of editing programs also offer the most flexibility when producing a video, and allow you to do pretty much whatever you can imagine if you have the patience and time to learn how to use them. It is important when considering one of these types of software programs to make sure your computer can handle what they require and again, understand they are not usually very intuitive. They take time to learn, sometimes even for the most basic task. If you choose this route – you are probably someone looking to produce videos for a living, some sort of financial gain – or you're a person who is really creative and likes to stretch your legs a bit when taking on something new. Most of these programs have free 30-day trials, so you can try them before you buy them. If the person I'm describing is not you – don't worry – there are other options.

If you still want to do the editing, but don't want to go down the rabbit hole the professional and even consumer versions of bigger editing programs offer – another option is an app on your phone or tablet. A popular program for Apple products is their program called iMovie. It functions in much the same way Final Cut Pro does (which is also an Apple product), but as you can imagine it is not nearly as robust. For about $5 to $15, you can download it and get to work. The videos it allows you to produce still look professional, and if you try to learn some of the more complex editing features it offers – you can really put something together that will make you or your team proud. iMovie also offers templates where you can simply add your footage, music and graphics / text, and presto, you've got a video. The drawback to these templates of course, is that they won't necessarily fit your ideas and footage perfectly. They are editable, meaning you can adjust them to a degree, but they will limit you a bit on what the final product will look like. If you don't like iMovie, or you have a product that isn't made by Apple, there are literally hundreds of other options for you to use. Even Adobe has one, which like iMovie, is a watered-down version of Premier Pro, called Adobe Premier Rush. Each one will have the ability to help you finish the video you've started. You'll just need to read through their descriptions and do your research to see which one best fits your needs. You may even want to download a few of them and compare that way.

Here is a link from Hubspot.com that goes through their top 20 picks for editing apps in 2020, have a look and see if any of these fit your needs:

https://blog.hubspot.com/marketing/best-video-editing-apps

Recently, several companies have popped up online offering editing services and that's it. They don't film, acquire footage, script or plan for you – they just take the footage you supply them with, and edit it to your specifications. In some cases, this can be quite expensive. But for shorter, simpler videos – these services can prove quite beneficial and affordable. First, you're getting a professional editor to work for you, which saves you time, and gives you the peace of mind that your final product will likely look good. The downside of this is that you're turning your project over to someone else, and when that happens, you're at their mercy and their rules. What might start off as an affordable process, could begin to become more and more costly as you request or need changes, or want to add a few bells and whistles. Add to that – that they may not be able to operate on your timeline, or even put together the project in a way you find satisfactory and you could end up with a big headache on your hands. My recommendation if you decide to go this route is to get everything in writing, do your homework on the company and make sure they are legitimate. Finally, find out if the editor who is working on your project is a person you can personally contact and correspond with. A better option might be to find a local video production company and see how they might be able to help you.

Lastly, there are websites and programs available (sometimes at quite affordable rates), which utilize templates and AI to create your video. One such service that I've used and been satisfied with is Animoto.com. Depending on what you need from them, they offer their services free (with their branding on the videos), on a per-video basis rate, and monthly or yearly subscriptions. They have several templates, which again allow you to insert your photos or videos, add graphics, your own music or music from their royalty-free library (we'll talk about royalty-free, what that means and why it's so important shortly), and basically press "go" and the video gets made. If you don't like what pops out – you can go back in and make any necessary changes and go again until you get a video you like. They even offer the option to create your videos in different resolutions and formats – so you can place them on Facebook, Instagram, Twitter and wherever else you'd like, in the style that best fits those programs. Animoto.com also offers you the ability to start from scratch and create the video however you'd like – with some limits as this service will not be as flexible as even a basic editing program. Similar programs that offer services along the same lines are Canva, Adobe Spark, Relay That (I have used and like each of these as well), and more. Just like everything else in the video creation process – it will be incumbent on you to do your research and find the solution that best suits your needs.

STOCK FOOTAGE, PHOTOS, AND MUSIC – ROYALTY FREE

As I mentioned previously, there are options out there that allow you to use stock video, photos, music, as well as video and graphics templates, among other products and services. These are all helpful in the video creation process. If you don't have the ability to go out and film / acquire your own assets for the video you're producing – this might be the route to go. When working for clients

– this option can save money and time for both of you as you don't have to spend the time filming, paying for actors and actresses, acquiring and paying for location permits and so on and so on. If you need a shot that features Mount Kilimanjaro from Africa, obviously, this is going to be MUCH easier than acquiring that shot on your own! The same goes for photos and music. The important part of these types of assets is that they are royalty free. Meaning you pay one time for the right to use them in your project, are given a license (make sure you read the license and ensure it covers what you're intending to use the video, music, or photo for), and you don't have to pay over and over to use the asset – even if your video blows up and goes viral making you millions of dollars. This is so important as many people learn the hard way that you can't just take an Elvis or Beattles' song and slap it into your video. Likewise, you can't take a clip from your favorite Hollywood blockbuster and put it into your video. If you do, just be prepared for a potential cease and desist letter or e-mail, and potentially a hefty fine to go with it.

Copyright laws don't allow you to just go grab a picture from Google Images, a song from iTunes, or a video from a movie, TV show, or use any celebrity images in your videos. If you're making a video, use these three questions when you're thinking of putting something in your video – no matter what it is:

1. Did you create it, or own it?
2. Did you get permission (in writing) to use it?
3. Did you purchase a license to use it?

If you can't answer a resounding "YES" to one of these three questions – DO NOT, I repeat, DO NOT use it! Especially if this is a video that is going to be made available for people to watch on social media or your website. If you do, you might get away with it for a while – but eventually, you'll be found out. Even if you don't get found out – ask yourself – would you want someone benefiting financially off something you put your talents, time and efforts into? If you wouldn't mind – you're a unicorn, and a better person than me!

# REVISIONS

Finally, after you've selected your video editing method, ensured that everything you're using is with permission and you've created a video to show your client or your team (or even just for yourself), be prepared for the requests for changes. It's going to happen – no matter how good your video is. It is rare that I create a video – even for myself – that no changes are requested. First things first – if you've followed this process and gotten everyone's approval before proceeding to the next step – the changes should be minimal. More like tweaks, rather than wholesale changes. The reason is as I stated at the beginning – they have been involved all along. They have added their input, which you've hopefully incorporated into the creation of what you're about to show them. If you did the script and shot list properly, or perhaps even created a storyboard, then the video has essentially already been seen. What you show them will not be a surprise, in fact, it will feel familiar! Secondly, don't take those requests for changes personally. If you've done your job – the client or team will likely be pleased with the video, but they need to have the final say. It's just the way it is. For some reason people just need to get that last bit of input out there before the project door closes. Just understand that changes are coming. Do your best to not let them hurt too much and get them done – even if they don't make the video better in your opinion. If you're being paid to make this video – that's your job. If it's just for you or your business – try not to be too critical of yourself. Do your best and keep practicing and creating. You will get better and better. And remember, George Lucas (known for going back and making changes) once said, "A famous filmmaker once said that films are never completed, they are only abandoned..."

## SOFTWARE RECOMMENDATIONS

### Editing Programs

- Adobe Premier Pro
- Vegas Pro
- Avid
- Final Cut Pro

### Editing Apps

- https://blog.hubspot.com/marketing/best-video-editing-apps

### Online Editing Services

- Video Husky
- Video Parachute
- Video Caddy

### Online Editors / Apps

- Animoto
- Adobe Spark
- Canva
- Relay That by AppSumo

# Step 6: Delivery

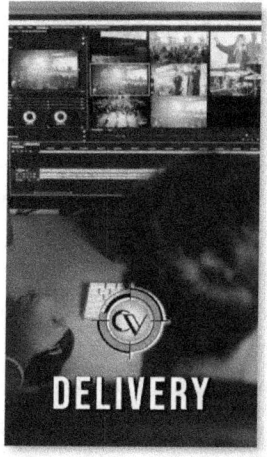

This section will be helpful in figuring out how to get the video you've just created to your client or team, as well as how you should render or export it based upon how they or you plan to use it.

Let's look at the intended use of the video. Most likely, if you've gotten this far – this is a video you or your client plans to use as a way of marketing or promoting themselves. If that's the case – there are a handful of ways the video can be completed.

First, however, let's get familiar with the video's aspect ratio / screen resolution – or the way it is viewed, along with its size and quality. This illustration will help you understand the terminology I'll be using in the next few sections.

**1280X720=720P**

**1920X1080=1080P**

**2560X1440=2.5K**

**THIS IMAGE IS 16X9**
16X9 REFERS TO THE ASPECT RATIO NUMBERS SUCH AS 1920X1080 REFER TO THE RESOLUTION OR SIZE/QUALITY

**4096X2160=4K**

If the video is primarily going to be used on a website, Facebook, YouTube, Vimeo, or perhaps even via an e-mail campaign – then the most likely way you'll need to render / export the video is in an HD format (either 1080p or 720p), which is 16x9 in its orientation (though eventually you will be able to utilize 4K, or UHD resolutions). Again, considering how you filmed it – the export needs to be in the same frame rate, or the video will have a weird look to it. So, if you filmed in 29.97 or 30 fps, make sure that matches in your render settings. The same goes for 23.976 or 24 fps. Some of the online services will only export at 30 fps – no matter what you upload to them – so just be aware of that or check to see if you can change their default settings!

**THIS IMAGE IS SQUARE, OR 1080X1080, THE SIZE USED ON INSTAGRAM POSTS**

When it comes to specific social media channels such as Instagram and Instagram TV, or even Twitter – the video will have to be rendered in a way that fits their formatting. For a regular Instagram video – the video must be rendered in a 1080x1080 (square) format and can be no longer than 1 minute, and a maximum size of 15mb. If the video is longer than 1 minute and is still being used on Instagram, you will have to use their option called Instagram TV. Instagram also offers "Stories" and "Reels" – which is the same formatting of Insta TV, but only 3 to 15 seconds in length. For the latter three, the video must be in a 9x16 format (the shape most cell phones are when held straight up and down). If you don't follow these guidelines and export it as 16x9 (1920x1080 or 1280x720 resolution), Instagram will crop the video and you will likely lose portions of the images and words you've included in the video.

**THIS IMAGE IS 9X16, THE SIZE USED ON INSTAGRAM TV, STORIES, & REELS**

With this in mind, you may have to go back to your editing software and do some cropping of your own to make sure words and images don't run off of the screen, or at least the most important parts of your video aren't cut off. If you're using a platform like Instagram and are filming with your phone – this might be when you just hold the phone straight up and down to get your footage, in order to avoid having to mess with it in post-production.

Twitter videos can use the 16x9 format, or 9x16 format (just like Instagram TV and Reels) and can accept videos up to 2 minutes and 20 seconds in length, with a maximum size of 512mb.

If you end up hiring an editor to take this on for you – simply let them know the places the video will be uploaded, and let them know you'd like them to fit the required formats of those channels and they should be able to care for that – though they may charge you a little extra to get it done. Otherwise, just adjust the settings in your software, app or online service to match the various requirements. More detailed specifications are listed at the end of this chapter.

As for an acceptable file format .MP4 is probably the most compatible format for all these channels when it comes to video. Others can include .AVI, .MOV, and .MP2.

Now that you've gone through the process of exporting the video in the desired formats – you'll need to get it to the customer, or your team. If you need to, you can copy the file to an external hard drive, USB drive, or deliver it via a cloud service such as Dropbox.com, Google Drive, or OneDrive. E-Mailing it likely won't work due to its size. Once in a blue moon you might still get a request for a DVD. If that's the case – you're going to need a DVD burner, blank DVDs, and a DVD authoring software (as for instructions – that's a different book, for a different time) One word of warning here – if you did this for pay – get your payment PRIOR to delivery. Once again, this is a painful lesson I've learned the hard way. Create a contract before work begins and write the contract this way. I even go as far to ask for 50% down, and 50% prior to final delivery. Most customers have no issue with this, and they completely understand. I'll include some necessities to include in your contract below.

VIDEO FORMATS (these can change with platform changes – so be sure to double check)

- Website, Facebook, YouTube, Vimeo: MP4, 16x9 (1920x1080 or 1280x720), Corresponding Frame Rate (Facebook will process the video down to 720p, but you can still upload 1080p)
- Instagram: MP4, 1080x1080, Corresponding Frame Rate, 3.5K Maximum Bitrate, 15 MB Maximum Size

- Instagram TV: MP4, 1080x1920, Corresponding Frame Rate, Maximum Length for uploading from a mobile device = 15 minutes, 60 minutes for uploading from the web
- Instagram Stories & Reels: MP4, 1080x1920, 3-15 seconds in Length, One Take or Edited, Mobile Only
- Twitter: MP4, 1920x1080, Corresponding Frame Rate, 2:20 Maximum Length, 512 MB Maximum Size

CONTRACT NECESSITIES

- A clear, defined product or end-result – what will be delivered and how.
- Describe EXACTLY what you'll be providing as a service, along with any equipment or extras.
- Describe EXACTLY what will be expected from the client.
- Define how many revisions the customer will be allowed, before overages kick in.
- Define what charges will be applied for overages, such as extra filming and editing beyond what is included.
- How much is required for a deposit (I recommend 50%, with the remaining balance due at delivery).
- Define any potential issues you can see arising – that may cause the project to grow – such as location fees, talent fees, licensing for b-roll and music, etc., and define who pays for what.
- If you can think of anything that can go wrong, or you've experienced in the past – put it in the contract.
- Finally, check with others, or even an attorney to make sure you've covered everything!

## Step 7: Distribution

If you've created this video for yourself, or if you'd like to help your client beyond just producing a video (and potentially earn yourself more work) – it is important to make sure the video actually gets seen.

As I said earlier, what good is a beautiful car with no engine? In this section, we're going to discuss some things you can do to make sure the video is actually seen. I'm not promising millions of views or a viral video if you follow these steps, but if you just slap it on your website and in a post on a social media channel or two – then you've wasted your time.

It is estimated that upwards of 80% of all internet traffic is video being downloaded, streamed or uploaded (which is just one reason you need to get a video done!). If that's the case – how in the world do you expect your video to be found and watched if you post it once or twice, and place it on your website? The short answer is – you shouldn't expect that at all. You might get a few views here and there – but the goal is to get a return on investment for your customers, clients, team or yourself. If you don't – your video career will be a short one. With that in mind – let's look at some things you can do organically or for no cost that will help your video get seen.

Let's start with placing it on YouTube or Vimeo. Most people don't place a video on their website directly anymore, at least they don't in my neck of the woods. The video is usually uploaded to YouTube or Vimeo and then embedded onto the website. If that's the case for you or your client, then there are some basic things you should do when you post to these video sites – even if it's not going on a website. You need to make it searchable. Therefore – when uploading and given the opportunity to title the video – come up with a title that is how you think people might search for it. Unless you or your client has a name or business name that everyone already knows and searches for – the best way to title the video is using some sort of search phrase. So, if you made a video to showcase how your widgets save time for a business – name it that way. Something like, "How to Save Time in Your Business with this Widget." Oftentimes using the phrase "How To" is immensely helpful as it is one of the most common beginnings to people's searches. If that won't work, consider using your location and what it is you offer. For example, "Kansas City Haunted House Attraction." However you decide to phrase it is up to you, but my suggestion is to consider how people are searching. You can put your business name in it as well – but find a way to incorporate it with the search phrase. If you can – try to keep the characters to around 130 characters or less. Titles that are too long just don't register as well.

Now for the description. This is the place to load up with more search phrases and keywords. For both YouTube and Vimeo, try to keep this area to around 5000 characters. Too short or too long and it won't register very well with search engines. Another good practice for businesses is to include the business name, address, phone number, e-mail and website EXACTLY as Google and other search engines see it at the bottom of your description. Something else that is handy is when adding the web address, if you use http:// followed by the website address instead of https://, the link will become clickable.

Tags are another necessity when uploading to YouTube and Vimeo. Again, think of keywords and phrases that you know people use to search for this product or service. If you're not sure what to use for the title, description or tags – simply search online for a free keyword tool. Google has one that is helpful, and obviously since they're the number one search engine – I'd highly recommend taking their suggestions. For YouTube there is no limit on how many tags you can use – but they do limit the space to 500 characters. Don't just fill up this section to fill it up. If you honestly can't find that many tags, just go with what you've got. Google owns YouTube and they are notorious for punishing people loading up on keywords just for the sake of doing it, by dropping them in the search rankings. Bonus tip for YouTube, again with Google owning YouTube, if you upload the video to YouTube, then embed it directly from YouTube to your website – you'll get some SEO (search engine optimization) brownie points, which will help in the search engine results when people are looking for you. For Vimeo you can use up to 20 tags, so if you can find that many, or come up with that many – go for it. Another, but more technical tip for YouTube is to upload the transcript of your video as well as filling out all the information regarding the video. It will require you basically typing out the wording in the video – but again this will help in search results. For how to do this – simply google the instructions, and you'll find the help you need.

If you're uploading the video to Instagram or Twitter, there are differences in how you go about getting it found. First, there is no option for titling the video – but you can still add a description. Instagram has a 2200-character limit. I wouldn't recommend filling this out entirely, but you can still use it to describe who you are and what you do, with use of keywords and phrases. You cannot place a website link in the Instagram description or comment area – but if there's a link you want people to go to you can use the famous "link in bio" line, and place the link in your Instagram bio. For Twitter, there is a 280-character limit – so you need to keep it short and sweet. You can post links for people to click on in Twitter, so if you'd like, direct them to your website or wherever you'd like them to go for information. You've probably also noticed on both platforms the use of hashtags or the # followed by a keyword or phrase. These are highly recommended as many people search both Instagram and Twitter by hashtags, just as much as they do by searching for people. Another benefit to using hashtags is that allows for the post to be indexed and placed in the Google search results. This allows people to find you while searching for these topics OUTSIDE of Instagram, Twitter, and Facebook. For Instagram, you can use a maximum of 30 hashtags, and if you've got the room – go ahead and use all 30. It can't hurt! Obviously, with Twitter your hashtags still need to fall in their 280-character limit. If you can, try to save room for three or four.

Moving onto Facebook. There isn't a lot of difference in what you do when posting a video than any other post to the platform. Facebook's post character limit is just over 63,000 – so you should be able to safely say what you want to without fear of going over. When you begin uploading your video to your business page it will ask for a title, a description, tags and a few other recommended spots to fill out to make the video easier to find. The reason for this is Facebook loves video, just like everyone else! So, fill it all out – it's only to your benefit. As for hashtags, again with a limit of 63,000 characters you can do almost as many as you like – but generally most people recommend 2 to 3, as this seems to work the best. Play around, do tests and see what works for you. Another easy way to get views on Facebook is if you placed the video on your business page, be sure to share it to your personal page. Then encourage other people to share it for you.

For all these platforms, you can examine analytics and see what is working and what isn't. Take advantage of that, and don't be afraid to post the video more than once. Just because you posted it at 10am on Monday doesn't mean all your customers and friends have seen it. Now don't go overboard and drive people nuts with it. Perhaps a couple of times a day at the most when you initially post it, and then perhaps a few other times here and there as long as it's relevant. Just don't do it so often that people don't want to see it anymore! Again, utilizing the analytics for each of these platforms will show you when is the best time to post it, how often it's being seen, and when it's starting to lose its effectiveness. Lastly, if people begin to share your post or comment on it – be sure to thank them in the comment section on your page or theirs, or like and respond to their comments on your post. This is just a good practice for businesses in general and will help you get seen by more eyes and show people you are responsive.

Another great place to post your videos, though you'll have to do it with a YouTube or Vimeo link, (especially for businesses) is LinkedIn. You can again create a post with commentary and hashtags (up to 700 characters) that will help the video be easier to discover – so take some time to get this done!

It seems like a new social media platform pops up every year or so that really takes off. Right now, it's TikTok. Next year it'll be something else. Do your homework and see if these other platforms are a good fit for you or your customers. Research the required video formats, character limits, tags and / or hashtags, and best practices for being discoverable, and you'll continue to find views for your video!

Videos can be highly effective in e-mail and marketing campaigns as well. There are a plethora of ways to send a video via e-mail, but the easiest way is to place a link from your website, YouTube, or Vimeo in the e-mail with a thumbnail image taken from the video (or even a gif if you know how to create one), along with some great copy. Studies show that videos cause click through rates on e-mails to go up significantly – so take some time to research the various ways you can do an e-mail blast or newsletter to your customers with your video. You can also purchase lists to e-mail to – though you really need to do your homework on the company supplying the list – as they can often be worthless (both the company and the lists). Regardless, find a way to get your video in an e-mail campaign and you might be pleasantly surprised with the results!

Last in the section, but not least, is your customer's or your website. I mentioned earlier there is a benefit to first uploading the video to

YouTube and then embedding the video into your site so that it is on your site but playing directly from YouTube. This will save bandwidth on your site from being used up – depending on the web hosting plan you have. YouTube will likely never be down, and it will play the file in HD. Finally, as I stated previously, YouTube is owned by Google, and Google will look favorably to you using their product on your website – especially if you've properly titled, described and tagged the video. If you do it all well, your website will rise in the Search Engine Results.

## BONUS Step 8: Ad Campaigns

Everything I've described in step 7 is organic in nature, meaning if done properly and with time, people will be able to find your video and hopefully view it – and all it will cost is your time. But let's face it – if you really want views and you want to maximize what the video can do for you – you must pay for it. Afterall, that's a big reason Google, YouTube, Vimeo, Instagram, Twitter, Facebook, LinkedIn – all of them - stay in business. There are ways you can learn tricks of the trade and do things to help your views and exposure grow – but without doubt – the quickest and most assured way to get a return on investment is to invest more.

We've all seen them...Ads. That's where it's at.

If you really want the video to be seen and become a sales tool for you – take some time and learn how to do Google Ads, YouTube Ads, and social media ads. These are great tools for targeting specific audiences, collecting potential customer information, on occasion a direct sale, and tracking what people are responding to. This type of work if you attempt to do it on your own, will require a lot of your time – as there is a lot of information to absorb. And like all technology it is everchanging in its nature. You can't just learn it one time and keep doing the same things, you'll always need to keep yourself updated on the new methods and techniques that come out as Google and the social media platforms update and improve on what they offer.

But I can say unequivocally that this works. Look at it this way...If someone expressed a sincere interest in working with you – what would you pay for the right to talk to them? $1, $2...Maybe $5? More? What would you pay if you knew the return on investment would be significant? That's what ads do for you. They put you in front of people who are interested in your product or service. Then – should they click on your ad – customers are directed to your website, phone number, or email.

Google Ads, YouTube Ads, and Social Media Ads help to eliminate some of the risk in advertising.

Traditional advertising has you pay for the ad and then pray the right people see or hear it. Google Ads and YouTube Ads eliminates some of that risk by ensuring people only see your advertisement when they search for you – or in the case of Social Media Ads – if they match the demographic you picked. So, you are marketing to who you want, where you want, and only to those searching for or have an interest in you. With Social Media Ads you select your campaign or daily budget, and you are almost guaranteed so many views based on what you spend – directly to the audience you select – down to their location, interests, and likes.

Again, if you're going to try to do this yourself – it will take some time and work to educate yourself to make sure you're not wasting your money. If that's not what you want to spend your time doing – I'd suggest finding someone who is an expert in these areas (eh-hem, www.cinematicvisions.com) to help you.


THE END.

# Thanks

Well, if you've made it this far – I'm sincerely flattered and appreciate you not only purchasing this book, but taking the time to read through my advice on what it takes to make a successful, professional looking video – as well as how to make sure it gets seen.

There are so many more things I could write about – but I wanted this to be a quick read, explaining things that can be intimidating in a clear and easy to understand way. Someday maybe I'll write a deeper more detailed book about the finer details of creating a video – but I didn't want to give away the store on my first outing!

Again, thank you for your time and business. I whole heartedly hope this information has proven to be helpful and has inspired you to give video a try. It simply is in my opinion, one of the most effective marketing tools available. If done well, it will help to grow your business and reach people in the way all studies show they prefer (7 out of 10 people prefer video to reading – look it up).

If I can be of any assistance to you – as I've mentioned a few times in this book you can reach me by going to my website at www.cinematicvisions.com, where you can e-mail or call. You can also find all my social media channels there. I'd love to connect with you and see any videos you make – so if you get one done – don't be afraid to tag me when you post it!

Thank you one more time and all the best to you and yours in everything you do.

Jeremy Wood, Cinematic Visions
www.cinematicvisions.com

Suggested Equipment Lists from Cinematic Visions:
https://www.amazon.com/shop/cinematicv

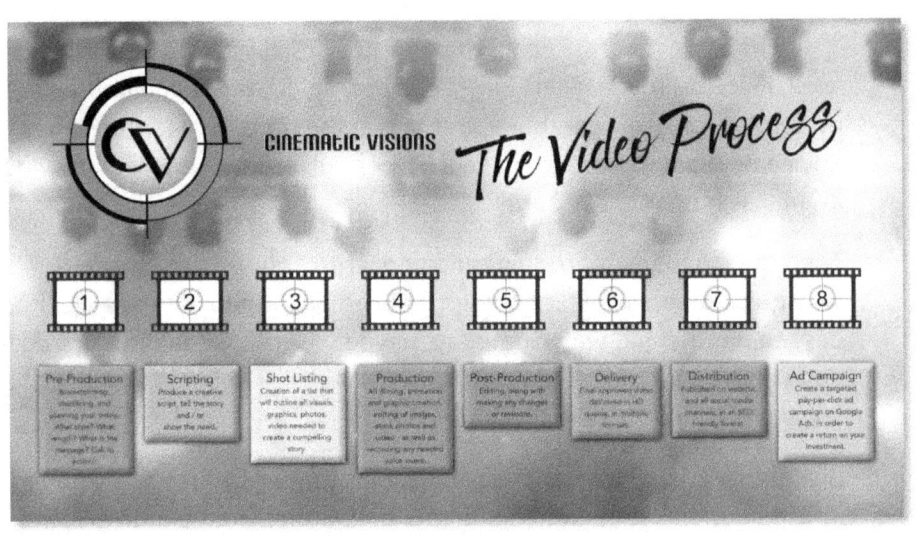

# HOW TO MAKE A

# PROFESSIONAL VIDEO

## IN 7 STEPS

### Jeremy Wood

**Cinematic Visions**

www.CinematicVisions.com